The Little Flowers of Saint Benedict

The Little Flowers of Saint Benedict

Gathered from the Dialogues
of Saint Gregory the Great

THE CENACLE PRESS
AT SILVERSTREAM PRIORY

This edition is based upon the 1901 edition of *The Little Flowers of St. Benet* with eight drawings and other designs throughout by Paul Woodroffe published by Kegan Paul, Trench Trubner & Co. Slight adaptations in spelling have been incorporated into the text.

Design of this edition is copyright ©
2023 by Silverstream Priory.

All rights reserved:
No part of this book may be reproduced or transmitted, in any form or by any means, without permission.

The Cenacle Press at Silverstream Priory
Silverstream Priory
Stamullen, County Meath, K32 T189, Ireland
www.cenaclepress.com

ppr 978-1-915544-74-2

Book design by Nora Malone

Cover design by Silverstream Priory

Cover art: Paul Woodroffe, *How Saint Benet passed away in his oratory*

Contents

Publisher's Note from the Original Edition xi

Introduction 1

I. How he made a broken sieve whole and sound 3

II. How he overcame a great temptation of the flesh . . . 9

III. How Benedict, by the sign of the holy cross,
brake a drinking-glass in pieces 13

IV. How Benedict reformed a monk that
would not stay at his prayers 19

V. Of a fountain that sprung forth on the top of a
mountain, by the prayers of the man of God 21

VI. How the iron head of a bill from the bottom
of the water returned to the handle again 23

VII. How Maurus walked upon the water 25

VIII. How a loaf was poisoned, and carried
far off by a crow. 29

IX. How venerable Benedict, by his prayer,
removed a huge stone 37

X. Of the fantastical fire which burned the
kitchen 39

XI. How venerable Benedict revived a boy
crushed to death with the ruin of a wall 41

XII. How by revelation venerable Benedict knew that
his monks had eaten out of the monastery 43

XIII. Of the brother of Valentinian the monk,
whom the man of God blamed for eating in
his journey. 45

XIV. How the dissimulation of King Totila was
discovered and found out by venerable
Benedict 49

XV. How venerable Benedict prophesied to
King Totila, and also to the Bishop of Canosa,
such things as were afterwards to fall out 53

XVI. Of a certain clergyman, whom venerable Benedict
for a time delivered from a devil. 55

XVII. How the man of God, Benedict, did foretell
the suppression of one of his own Abbeys 59

XVIII. How blessed Benedict knew the hiding away
of a flagon of wine. 61

XIX. How the man of God knew that one of his
monks had received certain handkerchiefs. . . . 63

XX. How holy Benedict knew the
proud thought of one of his monks 65

XXI. Of two hundred bushels of meal found
before the man of God's cell. 67

XXII. How by vision venerable Benedict disposed
the building of the Abbey of Terracina 69

XXIII. Of certain nuns absolved after their death. . . . 73

XXIV. Of a boy that after his burial was cast
out of his grave. 77

XXV. How a monk, forsaking the Abbey,
met with a dragon in the way 79

XXVI. How holy Benedict cured a boy of the
leprosy. 81

XXVII. How Benedict found money miraculously
to relieve a poor man 83

XXVIII. How a cruet of glass was thrown upon
the stones, and not broken. 85

XXIX. How an empty barrel was filled with oil 87

XXX. How Benedict delivered a monk from
a devil 89

XXXI. Of a country fellow, that, with the only sight of
the man of God, was loosed from his bonds . . 93

XXXII. How by prayer venerable Benedict raised up
a dead child. 97

XXXIII. Of a miracle wrought by his sister,
Scholastica 99

XXXIV. How Benedict saw the soul of his sister
ascend into heaven 103

XXXV. How he saw the whole world represented
before his eyes, and also the soul of Germanus,
Bishop of Capua, ascending to heaven 105

XXXVI. How holy Benedict
wrote a rule for his monks. 109

XXXVII. How venerable Benedict did prophesy to
his monks the time of his own death 111

XXXVIII. How a mad woman was cured in his cave . . 113

List of Illustrations

How St Benedict passed away in his oratory . . . . . cover

How St Benedict made a broken sieve whole. 7

How Brother Maurus walked on the water
    and saved Brother Placidus. 27

St Benedict commands the crow to carry away
    the poisoned loaf 35

How St Benedict quenched the fantastical fire. 40

How St Benedict discovered the deception
    of King Totila 51

How the devil disguised as a physician met
    St Benedict. 91

How St Benedict discoursed for the last time
    with St Scholastica 102

Publisher's Note from the Original Edition

St Benedict was born at Nursia, near Spoleto, in 480, and died on March 21, 543. His biography, as here printed, is taken from the second of the four books of "The Dialogues of S. Gregorie, surnamed the Great, Pope of Rome, and the first of that name. Translated into our English tongue, by P. W. Printed at Paris, 1608." The translator, P. W., has not been identified, though his version was twice reprinted during the last century. The present text follows that of the 1608 Edition, with which it has been collated, except in its spelling and the correction of one or two misprints.

Introduction

There was a man of venerable life, blessed by grace, and blessed in name—for he was called Benedictus, or Benedict—who, from his younger years, carried always the mind of an old man; for his age was inferior to his virtue. All vain pleasure he contemned; and though he were in the world, and might freely have enjoyed such commodities as it yieldeth, yet did he nothing esteem it, nor the vanities thereof. He was born in the province of Nursia, of honourable parentage, and brought up at Rome in the study of Humanity.

But, forasmuch as he saw many by reason of such learning to fall to dissolute and lewd life, he drew back his foot, which he had, as it were, now set forth into the world, lest entering too far into acquaintance therewith, he likewise might have fallen into that dangerous and godless gulf. Wherefore, giving over his books and forsaking his father's house and wealth, with a resolute mind only to serve God, he sought for some place where he might attain to the desire of his holy purpose: and in this sort he departed, instructed with learned ignorance, and furnished with unlearned wisdom. All the notable things and acts of his life I could not learn; but those few which I mind now to report, I had by the relation of four of his disciples, to wit, of Constantinus, a most rare and reverend man, who was next abbot after him; of Valentinianus, who many years had the charge of the Lateran Abbey; of Simplicius, who was the third General of his Order; and lastly, of Honoratus, who is now abbot of that monastery in which he first began his holy life.

✠

Chapter I

How he made a broken sieve whole and sound

Benedict, having now given over the school, with a resolute mind to lead his life in the wilderness, his nurse alone, which did tenderly love him, would not by any means give him over. Coming, therefore, to a place called Enside, and remaining there in the Church of St Peter in the company of other virtuous men, which for charity lived in that place, it fell so out that his nurse borrowed of the neighbours a sieve to make clean wheat, which, being left negligently upon the table, by chance it was broken in two pieces; whereupon she fell pitifully aweeping, because she had borrowed it. The devout and religious youth Benedict, seeing his nurse so lamenting, moved with compassion, took away with him both the pieces of the sieve, and with tears fell to his prayers; and after he had done, rising up, he found it so whole that the place could not be seen where before it was broken; and coming straight to his nurse, and comforting her with good words, he delivered her the sieve safe and sound; which miracle was known to all the inhabitants thereabouts, and so much admired that the townsmen, for a perpetual memory, did hang it up at the church door, to the end that not only men then living, but also their posterity, might understand how greatly God's grace did work with him upon his first renouncing of the world. The sieve continued there many years after, even to these very troubles of the Lombards, where it did hang over the church door.

But Benedict, desiring rather the miseries of the world than the praises of men, rather to be wearied with labour for God's sake than to be exalted with transitory commendation, fled privily from his nurse, and went into a desert place, called Subiaco, distant almost forty miles from Rome, in which there was a fountain springing forth cool and clear water, the abundance whereof doth first in a broad place make a lake, and afterwards, running forward, cometh to be a river. As he was travelling to this place, a certain monk, called Romanus, met him, and demanded whither he went; and, understanding his purpose, he both kept it close, furthered him what he might, vested him with the habit of holy conversation, and, as he could, did minister and serve him.

The man of God, Benedict, coming to this aforesaid place, lived there in a strait cave, where he continued three years, unknown to all men except to Romanus, who lived not far off, under the rule of Abbot Adeodatus, and very virtuously did steal certain hours, and likewise sometimes a loaf given for his own provision, which he did carry to Benedict. And because from Romanus' cell to that cave there was not any way, by reason of

How he made a broken sieve whole and sound

an high rock which did hang over it, Romanus, from the top thereof upon a long rope, did let down the loaf, upon which also with a band he tied a little bell, that by the ringing thereof the man of God might know when he came with his bread, and so be ready to take it; but the old enemy of mankind, envying at the charity of the one and the refection of the other, seeing a loaf upon a certain day let down, threw a stone, and brake the bell; but yet, for all that, Romanus gave not over to serve him by all the possible means he could.

At length, when Almighty God was determined to ease Romanus of his pains, and to have Benedict's life for an example known to the world, that such a candle, set upon a candlestick, might shine and give light to the Church of God, our Lord vouchsafed to appear unto a certain priest dwelling a good way off, who had made ready his dinner for Easter Day, and spake thus unto him: "Thou hast provided good cheer for thyself, and My servant in such a place is afflicted with hunger"; who, hearing this, forthwith rose up, and upon Easter Day itself, with such meat as he had prepared, went to the place, where he sought for the man of God amongst the steep hills, the low valleys, and hollow pits, and at length found him in his cave, where, after they had prayed together, and sitting down, had given God thanks, and had much spiritual talk, then the priest said unto him: "Rise up, brother, and let us dine, because today is the feast of Easter." To whom the man of God answered, and said: "I know that it is Easter with me, and a great feast, having found so much favour at God's hands as this day to enjoy your company" (for by reason of his long absence from men, he knew not that it was the great solemnity of Easter);

but the reverend priest again did assure him, saying: "Verily, today is the feast of our Lord's Resurrection; and therefore meet it is not that you should keep abstinence; and besides, I am sent to that end that we might eat together of such provisions as God's goodness hath sent us." Whereupon they said grace and fell to their meat; and after they had dined, and bestowed some time in talking, the priest returned to his church.

About the same time, likewise, certain shepherds found him in that same cave; and at the first, when they espied him through the bushes, and saw his apparel made of skins, they verily thought that it had been some beast: but after they were acquainted with the servant of God, many of them were, by his means, converted from their beastly life to grace, piety, and devotion. And thus his name in the country thereabout became famous, and many, after this, went to visit him, and for corporal meat, which they brought him, they carried away spiritual food for their souls.

How St Benedict made a broken sieve whole

✠

Chapter II

How he overcame a great temptation of the flesh

Upon a certain day, being alone, the tempter was at hand: for a little black bird, commonly called a merle, or an ousel, began to fly about his face, and that so near as the holy man, if he would, might have taken it with his hand: but after he had blessed himself with the sign of the cross the bird flew away: and forthwith the holy man was assaulted with such a terrible temptation of the flesh as he never felt the like in all his life.

A certain woman there was, which some time he had seen, the memory of which the wicked spirit put into his mind, and by the representation of her did so mightily inflame with concupiscence the soul of God's servant, which did so increase, that almost overcome with pleasure he was of mind to have forsaken the wilderness. But, suddenly assisted with God's grace, he came to himself; and seeing many thick briers and nettle-bushes to grow hard by, off he cast his apparel, and threw himself into the midst of them, and there wallowed so long, that when he rose up all his flesh was pitifully torn: and so by the wounds of his body he cured the wound of his soul, in that he turned pleasure into pain, and by the outward burning of extreme smart, quenched that fire which, being nourished before with the fuel of carnal cogitations, did inwardly burn in his soul: and by this means he overcame the sin because he made a change of the fire. From which time forward, as himself did afterward report unto his disciples, he found all temptation of pleasure so subdued, that he never felt any such thing.

Many after this began to abandon the world, and to become his scholars. For being now freed from the malady of temptation, worthily and with great reason is he made a master of virtue: for which cause, in Exodus, commandment is given by Moses, that the Levites from five-and-twenty years and upward should serve, but after they came to fifty that they should be ordained keepers of the holy vessels.

PETER. — Somewhat I understand of all this testimony alleged: but yet I beseech you to tell me the meaning thereof more fully.

GREGORY. — It is plain, Peter, that in youth the temptation of the flesh is hot: but after fifty years the heat of the body waxeth cold, and the souls of faithful people become holy vessels. Wherefore necessary it is that God's elect servants, whilst they are yet in the heat of temptation, should live in obedience, serve, and be wearied with labour and pains. But when, by reason of age, the heat of temptation is past, they become keepers of holy vessels because they then are made the doctors of men's souls.

How he overcame a great temptation of the flesh

PETER.—I cannot deny but that your words have given me full satisfaction: wherefore, seeing you have now explained the meaning of the former text alleged, prosecute, I pray, as you have begun, the rest of the holy man's life.

Chapter III

How Benedict, by the sign of the holy cross, brake a drinking-glass in pieces

GREGORY.—When this great temptation was thus overcome, the man of God, like unto a piece of ground well tilled and weeded, of the seed of virtue brought forth plentiful store of fruit: and by reason of the great report of his wonderful holy life, his name became very famous. Not far from the place where he remained there was a monastery, the Abbot whereof was dead: whereupon the whole Convent came unto the venerable man, Benedict, entreating him very earnestly that he would vouchsafe to take upon him the charge and government of their Abbey: long time he denied them, saying that their manners were diverse from his, and therefore that they should never agree together; yet at length, overcome with their entreaty, he gave his consent. Having now taken upon him the charge of the

The Little Flowers of Saint Benedict

Abbey, he took order that regular life should be observed, so that none of them could, as before they used, through unlawful acts decline from the path of holy conversation, either on the one side or on the other: which the monks perceiving, they fell into a great rage, accusing themselves that ever they desired him to be their abbot, seeing their crooked conditions could not endure his virtuous kind of government: and therefore when they saw that under him they could not live in unlawful sort, and were loath to leave their former conversation, and found it hard to be enforced with old minds to meditate and think upon new things, and because the life of virtuous men is always grievous to those that be of wicked conditions, some of them began to devise how they might rid him out of the way: and therefore, taking counsel together, they agreed to poison his wine: which being done, and the glass wherein that wine was, according to the custom, offered to the Abbot to bless, he, putting forth his hand, made the sign of the cross, and straightway the glass, that was holden far off, brake in pieces, as though the sign of the cross had been a stone thrown against it: upon which accident the man of God by-and-by perceived that the glass had in it the drink of death, which could not endure the sign of life: and therefore rising up, with a mild countenance and quiet mind he called the monks together, and spake thus unto them: "Almighty God have mercy upon you, and forgive you: why have you used me in this manner? Did not I tell you beforehand, that our manner of living could never agree together? Go your ways, and seek ye out some other Father suitable to your own conditions, for I intend not now to stay any longer amongst you."

How Benedict brake a drinking-glass in pieces

When he had thus discharged himself, he returned back to the wilderness which he so much loved, and dwelt alone with himself, in the sight of his Creator, Who beholdeth the hearts of all men.

PETER.—I understand not very well what you mean, when you say that he dwelt with himself.

GREGORY.—If the holy man had longer, contrary to his own mind, continued his government over those monks, who had all conspired against him, and were far unlike to him in life and conversation, perhaps he should have diminished his own devotion, and somewhat withdrawn the eyes of his soul from the light of contemplation; and being weary daily with correcting of their faults, he should have had the less care of himself, and so haply it might have fallen out that he should both have lost himself, and yet not found them: for so often as by infectious motion we are carried too far from ourselves, we remain the same men that we were before, and yet be not with ourselves as we were before: because we are wandering about other men's affairs, little considering and looking into the state of our own soul. For shall we say that he was with himself, who went into a far country, and after he had, as we read in the Gospel,[1] prodigally spent that portion which he received of his father, was glad to serve a citizen, to keep his hogs, and would willingly have filled his hungry belly with the husks which they did eat? Who, notwithstanding, afterward when he thought with himself of those goods which he had lost, it is written of him, that returning into himself, he said: "How many hired men in my father's house do abound with bread!" If,

---

[1] Luke xv.

then, before he were with himself, from whence did he return home unto himself? And therefore I said that this venerable man did dwell with himself, because, carrying himself circumspectly and carefully in the sight of his Creator, always considering his own actions, always examining himself, never did he turn the eyes of his soul from himself to behold aught else whatsoever.

PETER.—Why, then, is it written of the Apostle, St Peter, after he was by the Angel delivered out of prison, that returning to himself, he said: "Now I know verily, that our Lord has sent His Angel, and hath delivered me from the hands of Herod, and from all the expectation of the people of the Jews?"[2]

GREGORY.—We are two manner of ways, Peter, carried out of ourselves: for either we fall under ourselves by sinful cogitation, or else we are, by the grace of contemplation, lifted above ourselves: for he that kept hogs, through wandering of his mind and unclean thoughts fell under himself: but he whom the Angel delivered out of prison, being also rapt by the Angel into an ecstasy, was in truth out of himself, but yet above himself. Both of them, therefore, did return unto themselves; the one when he recollected himself, and forsook his lewd kind of life; and the other from the top of contemplation to have that usual judgment and understanding which before he had: wherefore venerable Benedict in that solitary wilderness dwelt with himself, because he kept himself, and retired his cogitations within the closet of his own soul: for when the greatness of contemplation rapt him up aloft, out of all question he did then leave himself under himself.

---

[2] Acts xii.

How Benedict brake a drinking-glass in pieces

PETER.—Your discourse doth very well content me, yet I beseech you to answer me this question; whether he could in conscience give over those monks, whose government he had now taken upon him?

GREGORY.—In mine opinion, Peter, evil men may with good conscience be tolerated in that community where there be some good that may be holpen, and reap commodity. But where there be none good at all, that may receive spiritual profit, oftentimes all labour is lost that is bestowed in bringing of such to good order, especially if other occasions be offered of doing God presently better service elsewhere: for whose good, then, should the holy man have expected, seeing them all to persecute him with one consent? And (that which is not to be passed over with silence) those that be perfect carry always this mind, that when they perceive their labour to be fruitless in one place, to remove straight to another, where more good may be done. And for this cause, that notable preacher of the world, who was desirous to be dissolved, and to be with Christ, unto whom "to live is Christ; and to die is gain,"[3] and who not only desired himself to suffer persecution, but did also animate and encourage others to suffer the same, yet being himself in persecution at Damascus, got a rope and a basket to pass over the wall, and was privily let down. What then? Shall we say that Paul was afraid of death, whenas himself said that he desired it for Christ's sake? Not so: but when he perceived that in that place little good was to be done by great labour, he reserved himself to further labour, where more fruit

---

[3] Philipp. i. 21.

and better success might be expected: and therefore the valiant soldier of Christ would not be kept within walls, but sought for a larger field where he might more freely labour for his Master. And so, in like manner, you shall quickly perceive, if you mark well, that venerable Benedict forsook not so many in one place, that were unwilling to be taught, as he did in sundry other places raise up from the death of soul many more that were willing to be instructed.

PETER.—It is so as you say, and plain reason teacheth it, and the example of St Paul doth confirm it. But I beseech you to return unto your former purpose, and to prosecute the life of the holy man.

GREGORY.—Whenas God's servant daily increased in virtue, and became continually more famous for miracles, many were by him in the same place drawn to the service of Almighty God, so that by Christ's assistance he built there twelve Abbeys, over which he appointed governors, and in each of them he placed twelve monks; and a few he kept with himself, namely, such as he thought would more profit, and be better instructed by his own presence. At that time, also, many noble and religious men of Rome came unto him, and committed their children to be brought up under him, for the service of God. Then also Aequitius delivered him Maurus, and Tertullus the Senator brought Placidus, being their sons of great hope and towardness, of which two, Maurus, growing to great virtue, began to be his master's coadjutor; but Placidus, as yet, was but a boy of tender years.

✠

Chapter IV

How Benedict reformed a monk that would not stay at his prayers

In one of the monasteries which he had built in those parts, a monk there was which could not continue at prayers; for when the other monks knelt down to serve God, his manner was to go forth, and there with wandering mind to busy himself about some earthly and transitory things. And when he had been often by his Abbot admonished of this fault without any amendment, at length he was sent to the man of God, who did likewise very much rebuke him for his folly; yet notwithstanding, returning back again, he did scarce two days follow the holy man's admonition; for upon the third day he fell again to his old custom, and would not abide within at the time of prayer; word whereof being once more sent to the man of God, by the father of the Abbey whom he had there appointed, he returned him answer that he would come himself and reform what was amiss which he did accordingly, and it so fell out that when the singing of psalms was ended, and the hour come in which the monks betook themselves to prayer, the holy man perceived that the monk, which used at that time to go forth, was by a little black boy drawn out by the skirt of his garment, upon which sight he spake secretly to Pompeianus, father of the Abbey, and also to Maurus, saying: "Do you not see who it is that draweth this monk from his prayers?" and they answered him that they did not. "Then let us pray," quoth he, "that you also may behold whom this monk doth follow"; and after two days Maurus did see him, but Pompeianus could not. Upon another day, when the man of God had ended his devotions, he went out of the oratory, where he found the aforesaid monk standing idle, whom for the blindness of his heart he struck with a little wand, and from that day forward he was so freed from all allurement of the little black boy, that he remained quietly at his prayers, as others of the monks did, for the old enemy was so terrified, that he durst not any more suggest any such cogitations: as though by that blow not the monk, but himself had been stricken.

✠

Chapter V

Of a fountain that sprung forth on the top of a mountain, by the prayers of the man of God

Amongst the monasteries which he had built in those parts, three of them were situated upon the rocks of a mountain; so that very painful it was for the monks to go down and fetch water, especially because the side of the hill was so steep that there was great fear of danger; and therefore the monks of those Abbeys with one consent came unto the servant of God, Benedict, giving him to understand how laborious it was for them daily to go down unto the lake for water: and therefore they added that it was very necessary to have them removed to some other places. The man of God, comforting them with sweet words, caused them to return back again; and the next night, having with him only the little boy Placidus (of whom we spake before), he ascended up to the rock of that mountain, and continued there a long time in prayer: and when he had done, he took three stones and laid them in the same place for a mark; and so, none of them being privy to that he had done, he returned back to his own Abbey, and the next day, when the aforesaid monks came again about their former business, he said thus unto them: "Go your way to the rock, and in the place where you find three stones laid one upon another, dig a little hole, for Almighty God is able to bring forth water in the top of that mountain, and so to ease you of that great labour which you take in fetching it so far." Away they went, and came to the rock of that mountain according to his direction, which they found, as it were, sweating drops of water, and after they had with a spade made a hollow place, it was straightway filled, and water flowed out so abundantly, that it doth plentifully, even to this day, spring out and run down from the top to the very bottom of that hill.

Chapter VI

How the iron head of a bill from the bottom of the water returned to the handle again

At another time, a certain Goth, poor of spirit, that gave over the world, was received by the man of God, whom one day he commanded to take a bill, and to cleanse a certain plot of ground from briers, for the making of a garden; which ground was by the side of a lake. The Goth, as he was there labouring, by chance the head of the bill slipped off, and fell into the water, which was so deep that there was no hope ever to get it again. The poor Goth, in great fear, ran unto Maurus, and told him what he had lost, confessing his own fault and negligence. Maurus forthwith went to the servant of God, giving him to understand thereof, who came straightway to the lake, and took the handle out of the Goth's hand, and put it into the water, and the iron head, by-and-by, ascended from the bottom and entered into the handle of the bill, which he delivered to the Goth, saying: "Behold, here is thy bill again, work on and be sad no more."

Chapter VII

How Maurus walked upon the water

On a certain day, as venerable Benedict was in his cell, the aforesaid young Placidus, the holy man's monk, went out to take up water at the lake, and putting down his pail, carelessly, fell in himself after it, whom the water forthwith carried away from the land so far as one may shoot an arrow. The man of God, being in his cell, by-and-by knew this, and called in haste for Maurus, saying: "Brother Maurus, run as fast as you can, for Placidus, that went to the lake to fetch water, is fallen in, and is carried a good way off." A strange thing, and since the time of Peter the Apostle never heard of! Maurus, craving his father's blessing, and departing in all haste at his commandment, ran to the place upon the water, to which the young lad was carried by force thereof, thinking that he had all that while gone upon the land: and taking fast hold of him by the hair of his head, in all haste he returned back again: and so soon as he was at land, coming to himself, he looked behind him, and then knew very well that he had before run upon the water: and that which before he durst not have presumed, being now done and past, he both marvelled, and was afraid at that which he had done. Coming back to the father, and telling him what had happened, the venerable man did not attribute this to his own merits but to the obedience of Maurus: but Maurus, on the contrary, said that it was done only upon his commandment, and that he had nothing to do in that miracle, not knowing at that time what he did. But the friendly contention proceeding of mutual humility, the young youth himself that was saved from drowning did determine: for he said that he saw when he was drawn out of the water, the Abbot's garment upon his head, affirming that it was he that had delivered him from that great danger.

Peter. — Certainly they be wonderful things which you report, and such as may serve for the edification of many: for mine own part, the more that I hear of his miracles, the more do I still desire.

How Brother Maurus walked on the water and saved Brother Placidus

✠

Chapter VIII

How a loaf was poisoned, and carried far off by a crow

Whenas the aforesaid monasteries were zealous in the love of our Lord Jesus Christ, and their fame dispersed far and near, and many gave over the secular life, and subdued the passions of their soul under the light yoke of our Saviour, then (as the manner of wicked people is to envy at that virtue which themselves desire not to follow), one Florentius, priest of a church hard by, and grandfather to Florentius, our sub-deacon, possessed with diabolical malice, began to envy the holy man's virtues, to backbite his manner of living, and to withdraw as many as he could from going to visit him; and when he saw that he could not hinder his virtuous proceedings, but that, on the contrary, the fame of his holy life increased, and many daily, upon the very report of his sanctity, did betake themselves to a better state of life: burning more and more with the coals of envy, he became far worse; and though he desired not to imitate his commendable life, yet fain he would have had the reputation of his virtuous conversation. In conclusion, so much did malicious envy blind him, and so far did he wade in that sin, that he poisoned a loaf, and sent it to the servant of Almighty God, as it were for an holy present. The man of God received it with great thanks, yet not ignorant of that which was hidden within. At dinner-time, a crow daily used to come unto him from the next wood, which took bread at his hands; coming that day after his manner, the man of God threw him the loaf which the priest had sent him, giving him this charge: "In the Name of Jesus Christ, our Lord, take up that loaf, and leave it in some such place where no man may find it." Then the crow, opening his mouth, and lifting up his wings, began to hop up and down about the loaf, and after his manner to cry out, as though he would have said that he was willing to obey, and yet could not do what he was commanded. The man of God again and again bade him, saying: "Take it up without fear, and throw it where no man may find it." At length, with much ado, the crow took it up and flew away; and after three hours, having despatched the loaf, he returned back again, and received his usual allowance from the man of God.

But the venerable father perceiving the priest so wickedly bent against his life, was far more sorry for him than grieved for himself. And Florentius, seeing that he could not kill the body of the master, laboureth now what he can to destroy the souls of his disciples; and for that purpose he sent into the yard of the abbey before their eyes seven naked young women, which did there take hands together, play, and dance a long time before them:

How a loaf was poisoned, and carried far off by a crow

to the end that by this means they might inflame their minds to sinful lust: which damnable sight the holy man beholding out of his cell, and fearing the danger which thereby might ensue to his younger monks, and considering that all this was done only for the persecuting of himself, he gave place to envy; and therefore, after he had for those abbeys and oratories which he had there built appointed governors, and left some under their charge, himself, in the company of a few monks, removed to another place.

And thus the man of God, upon humility, gave place to the other's malice; but yet Almighty God of justice did severely punish his wickedness. For when the aforesaid priest, being in his chamber understood of the departure of holy Benedict, and was very glad of that news, behold (the whole house besides continuing safe and sound) that chamber alone in which he was fell down, and so killed him: which strange accident the holy man's disciple, Maurus, understanding, straightway sent him word, he being as yet scarce ten miles off, desiring him to return again, because the priest that did persecute him was slain; which thing when Benedict heard, he was passing sorrowful, and lamented much, both because his enemy died in such sort, and also for that one of his monks rejoiced thereat, and therefore he gave him penance, for that sending such news, he presumed to rejoice at his enemy's death.

PETER.—The things you report be strange, and much to be wondered at: for in making the well to yield forth water, I see Moses; and in the iron which came from the bottom of the lake I behold Eliseus; in the walking of Maurus upon the water I perceive Peter; in the obedience of the crow I contemplate Elias;

and in the lamenting the death of his enemy I acknowledge David; and therefore, in mine opinion, this one man was full of the spirit of all good men.

GREGORY.—The man of God, Benedict, had the spirit of the One True God, Who, by the grace of our redemption, hath filled the hearts of His elect servants; of Whom St John saith: "He was the True Light, which doth lighten every man coming into this world."[4] Of Whom again we find it written: "Of His fulness we have all received."[5] For God's holy servants might receive virtues of our Lord, but to bestow them upon others they could not; and therefore it was He that gave the signs of miracles to His servants, Who promised to give the sign of Jonas to His enemies[6]: so that He vouchsafed to die in the sight of the proud, and to rise again before the eyes of the humble: to the end that they might behold what they contemned, and thus see that which they ought to worship and love: by reason of which mystery it cometh to pass that whereas the proud cast their eyes upon the contempt of His Death, the humble contrariwise, against death, lay hold of the glory of His power and might.

PETER.—To what places, I pray you, after this, did the holy man go: and whether did he afterwards in them work any miracles, or no?

GREGORY.—The holy man, changing his place, did not, for all that, change his enemy. For afterwards he endured so much the

---

[4] 1 John i.
[5] John i.
[6] Matt. vii. 20.

How a loaf was poisoned, and carried far off by a crow

more grievous battles, by how much he had now the Master of all wickedness fighting openly against him. For the town, which is called Cassino, standeth upon the side of a high mountain, which containeth, as it were in the lap thereof, the aforesaid town, and afterward so riseth in height for the space of three miles, that the top thereof seemeth to touch the very heavens: in this place there was an ancient chapel in which the foolish and simple country people, according to the custom of the old Gentiles, worshipped the god Apollo. Round about it likewise upon all sides there were woods for the service of the devils, in which, even to that very time, the mad multitude of infidels did offer most wicked sacrifice. The man of God coming thither, beat in pieces the idol, overthrew the altar, set fire to the woods, and in the temple of Apollo he built the oratory of St Martin: and where the altar of the same Apollo was he made an oratory of St John: and by his continual preaching he brought the people dwelling in those parts to embrace the faith of Christ. The old enemy of mankind, not taking this in good part, did, not now privily or in a dream, but in open sight, present himself to the eyes of that holy father, and with great outcries complained that he had offered him violence. The noise which he made the monks did hear, but himself they could not see: but as the venerable father told them he appeared visibly unto him most fell and cruel, and as though, with his fiery mouth and flaming eyes, he would have torn him in pieces: what the devil said unto him all the monks did hear; for first he would call him by his name, and because the man of God vouchsafed him not any answer, then would he fall a reviling and railing at him: for when he cried out, calling him "Blessed Benedict" and yet found that he gave him no answer, straightway he would turn his tune, and say: "Cursed Benedict, and not blessed: what hast thou to do with me? And why dost thou thus persecute me?" Wherefore new battles of the old enemy against the servant of God are to be looked for, against whom willingly did he make war, but against his will did he give him occasion of many notable victories.

St Benedict commands the crow to carry away the poisoned loaf

Chapter IX

How venerable Benedict, by his prayer, removed a huge stone

Upon a certain day, when the monks were building up the cells of the same Abbey, there lay a stone which they meant to employ about that business: and when two or three were not able to remove it, they called for more company; but all in vain, for it remained so immovable as though it had grown to the very earth; whereby they plainly perceived that the devil himself did sit upon it, seeing so many men's hands could not so much as once move it: wherefore, finding that their own labours could do nothing, they sent for the man of God, to help them with his prayers against the devil, who hindered the removing of that stone. The holy man came: and after some praying he gave it his blessing, and then they carried it away so quickly as though it had been of no weight at all.

Chapter X

Of the fantastical fire which burned the kitchen

Then the man of God thought good that they should presently before his departure dig up the ground in the same place; which being done, and a deep hole made, the monks found there an idol of brass, which being for a little while by chance cast into the kitchen, they beheld fire suddenly to come from it, which to all their sight seemed to set the whole kitchen on fire: for the quenching whereof, the monks by casting on of water made such a noise, that the man of God hearing it came to see what the matter was: and himself beholding not any fire at all, which they said that they did, he bowed down his head forthwith to his prayers; and then he perceived that they were deluded with fantastical fire; and therefore bade them bless their eyes, that they might behold the kitchen safe and sound, and not those fantastical flames which the devil had falsely devised.

How St Benedict quenched the fantastical fire

✠

Chapter XI

How venerable Benedict revived a boy crushed to death with the ruin of a wall

Again, as the monks were making of a certain wall somewhat higher, because that was requisite, the man of God in the meantime was in his cell at his prayers. To whom the old enemy appeared in an insulting manner, telling him, that he was now going to his monks, that were aworking; whereof the man of God in all haste gave them warning, wishing them to look unto themselves, because the devil was at that time coming amongst them. The message was scarce delivered, whenas the wicked spirit overthrew the new wall which they were abuilding, and with the fall slew a little young child, a monk, who was the son of a certain courtier. At which pitiful chance all were passing sorry and exceedingly grieved, not so much for the loss of the wall, as for the death of their brother: and in all haste they sent

The Little Flowers of Saint Benedict

the heavy news to the venerable man Benedict; who commanded them to bring unto him the young boy, mangled and maimed as he was: which they did, but yet they could not carry him any otherwise than in a sack: for the stones of the wall had not only broken his limbs, but also his very bones. Being in that manner brought unto the man of God, he bade them to lay him in his cell, and in that place upon which he used to pray; and then putting them all forth, he shut the door, and fell more instantly to his prayers than he used at other times. And O strange miracle! For the very same hour he made him sound, and as lively as ever he was before; and sent him again to his former work, that he also might help the monks to make an end of that wall, of whose death the old serpent thought he should have insulted over Benedict, and greatly triumphed.

✠

Chapter XII

How by revelation venerable Benedict knew that his monks had eaten out of the monastery

Among other miracles which the man of God did, he began also to be famous for the spirit of prophecy: as to foretell what was to happen, and to relate unto them that were present such things as were done in his absence. The order of his Abbey was, when the monks went abroad (to deliver any message) never to eat or drink anything out of their cloister: and this being diligently observed, according to the prescription of their rule, upon a certain day, some of the monks went forth upon such business: and being enforced about the despatch thereof to tarry somewhat long abroad, it so fell out that they stayed at the house of a religious woman, where they did eat and refresh themselves. And being late before they came back to the Abbey, they went, as the manner was, and asked their father's blessing: of whom he demanded where they had eaten, and they said "nowhere." "Why do you," quoth he, "tell an untruth? For did you not go into such a woman's house, and eat such and such kind of meat, and drink so many cups?" When they heard him recount so in particular, both where they had stayed, what kind of meat they had eaten, and how often they had drunk; and perceived well that he knew all whatsoever they had done, they fell down trembling at his feet, and confessed that they had done wickedly: who straightway pardoned them for that fault, persuading himself that they would not any more in his absence presume to do any such thing, seeing they now perceived that he was present with them in spirit.

✠

Chapter XIII

Of the brother of Valentinian the monk, whom the man of God blamed for eating in his journey

A brother also of Valentinian the monk, of whom I made mention before, was a layman, but devout and religious: who used every year, as well to desire the prayers of God's servant, as also to visit his natural brother, to travel from his own house to the Abbey: and his manner was, not to eat anything all that day before he came thither. Being therefore, upon a time, in his journey, he lighted into the company of another that carried meat about him to eat by the way: who, after the day was well spent, spake unto him in this manner: "Come, brother," quoth he, "let us refresh ourselves, that we faint not in our journey": to whom he answered: "God forbid: for eat I will not by any means, seeing I am now going to the venerable father, Benedict, and my custom is to fast until I see him." The other, upon this answer, said no more for the space of an hour: but afterwards, having travelled a little further, again he was in hand with him to eat something: yet then likewise he utterly refused, because he meant to go through fasting as he was. His companion was content, and so went forward with him, without taking anything himself. But when they had now gone very far and were well wearied with long travelling, at length they came unto a meadow, where there was a fountain, and all such other pleasant things as use to refresh men's bodies.

Then his companion said to him again: "Behold here is water, a green meadow, and a very sweet place, in which we may refresh ourselves, and rest a little, that we may be the better able to despatch the rest of our journey"; which kind words bewitching his ears, and the pleasant place flattering his eyes, content he was to yield unto the motion, and so they fell to their meat together: and coming afterward in the evening to the Abbey, they brought him to the venerable father, Benedict, of whom he desired his blessing. Then the holy man objected against him what he had done in the way, speaking to him in this manner: "How fell it out, brother," quoth he, "that the devil talking to you by means of your companion, could not at the first nor second time persuade you: but yet he did at the third, and made you do what best pleased him?"

The good man, hearing these words, fell down at his feet, confessing the fault of his frailty; and was grieved, and so much the more ashamed of his sin, because he perceived that though he were absent, that yet he did offend in the sight of that venerable father.

Of the brother of Valentinian the monk

PETER.—I see well that the holy man had in his soul the spirit of Eliseus, who was present with his servant, Giezi, being then absent from him.

✠

Chapter XIV

How the dissimulation of King Totila was discovered and found out by venerable Benedict

GREGORY.—You must, good Peter, for a little while be silent, that you may know matters yet far more important. For in the time of the Goths, when Totila, their king, understood that the holy man had the spirit of prophecy, as he was going towards his monastery, he remained in a place somewhat far off, and beforehand sent the father word of his coming; to whom answer was returned that he might come at his pleasure. The king, as he was a man wickedly disposed, thought he would try whether the man of God were a prophet, as it was reported, or no. A certain man of his guard he had, called Riggo, upon whom he caused his own shoes to be put, and to be apparelled with his other princely robes, commanding him to go, as it were himself, to the man of God; and to give the better colour to this device, he sent three to attend upon him who especially were always about the king, to wit, Vuldericus, Rudericus, and Blindinus; charging them, that in the presence of the servant of God, they should be next about him, and behave themselves in such sort as though he had been King Totila indeed: and that diligently they should do unto him all other services, to the end that both by such dutiful kind of behaviour, as also by his purple robes, he might verily be taken for the king himself. Riggo, furnished with that brave apparel, and accompanied with many courtiers, came unto the Abbey: at which time the man of God sat a little way off, and when Riggo was come so near that he might well understand what the man of God said, then, in the hearing of them all, he spake thus: "Put off, my good son, put off that apparel, for that which thou hast on is none of thine." Riggo, hearing this, fell straightway down to the ground, and was very much afraid, for presuming to go about to mock so worthy a man: and all his attendants and servitors fell down likewise to the earth, and after they were up again they durst not approach any nearer to his presence; but returned back to their king, telling him with fear, how quickly they were discovered.

How St Benedict discovered the deception of King Totila

✠

Chapter XV

How venerable Benedict prophesied to King Totila, and also to the Bishop of Canosa, such things as were afterwards to fall out

Then Totila himself, in person, went unto the man of God; and seeing him sitting afar off, he durst not come near, but fell down to the ground; whom the holy man (speaking to him twice or thrice) desired to rise up, and at length came unto him, and with his own hands lifted him up from the earth where he lay prostrate: and then, entering into talk, he reprehended him for his wicked deeds, and in few words told him all that which should befall him, saying: "Much wickedness do you daily commit, and many great sins have you done: now at length give over your sinful life. Into the city of Rome shall you enter, and over the sea shall you pass: nine years shall you reign, and in the tenth shall you leave this mortal life." The King, hearing these things, was wonderfully afraid, and desiring the holy man to commend him to God in his prayers, he departed: and from that time forward he was nothing so cruel as before he had been. Not long after he went to Rome, sailed over into Sicily, and in the tenth year of his reign he lost his kingdom together with his life.

The Bishop also of Canosa used to visit the servant of God, whom the holy man dearly loved for his virtuous life. The Bishop, therefore, talking with him of King Totila, of his taking of Rome, and the destruction of that city, said: "This city will be so spoiled and ruined by him that it will never be more inhabited." To whom the man of God answered: "Rome," quoth he, "shall not utterly be destroyed by strangers, but shall be so shaken with tempest, lightnings, whirlwinds, and earthquakes, that it will fall to decay of itself." The mysteries of which prophecy we now behold as clear as the day: for we see before our eyes in this very city by a strange whirlwind the world shaken, houses ruined, and churches overthrown, and buildings rotten with old age we behold daily to fall down. True it is that Honoratus, by whose relation I had this, saith not that he received it from his own mouth, but that he had it of other monks, which did hear it themselves.

✠

Chapter XVI

Of a certain clergyman, whom venerable Benedict for a time delivered from a devil

At the same time, a certain clergyman, that served in the church of Aquinum, was possessed: whom the venerable man, Constantius, Bishop of the same city, sent unto many places of holy martyrs for help: but God's holy martyrs would not deliver him, to the end that the world might know what great grace was in the servant of God, Benedict; wherefore at length he was brought unto him, who, praying for help to Jesus Christ, our Lord, did forthwith cast the old enemy out of the possessed man's body, giving him this charge: "Go your way, and hereafter abstain from eating of flesh, and presume not to enter into holy orders, for whensoever you shall attempt any such thing, the devil again will have power over you." The man departed safe and sound, and because punishment fresh in memory useth to terrify the mind, he observed for a time what the man of God had given him in commandment. But after many years, when all his seniors were dead, and he saw his juniors preferred before him to holy orders, he neglected the words of the man of God, as though forgotten through length of time, and took upon him holy orders: whereupon straightway the devil, that before had left him, entered again, and never gave over to torment him until he had separated his soul from his body.

PETER.—This holy man, as I perceive, did know the secret counsel of God: for he saw that this clergyman was delivered to the power of the devil, to the end he should not presume to enter into holy orders.

GREGORY.—Why should he not know the secrets of God who kept the commandments of God: whereas the Scripture saith: "He that cleaveth unto our Lord is one spirit, with Him."[7]

PETER.—If he that cleaveth unto our Lord be one spirit with our Lord, what is the meaning of that which the Apostle saith: "Who knoweth the sense of our Lord, or who hath been His counsellor?"[8] for it seemeth very inconvenient to be ignorant of His sense, to whom being so united he is made one thing.

GREGORY.—Holy men, in that they be one with our Lord, are not ignorant of His sense: for the same Apostle saith: "For what man knoweth those things which belong to man, but the spirit of man which is in him.[9] Even so, the things which belong to God

---

[7] 1 Cor. vi.

[8] 2 Rom. xi.

[9] 1 Cor. ii.

Of a clergyman, whom Benedict delivered from a devil

no man knoweth but the Spirit of God"[10]: and to show also that he knew such things as belong to God, he added straight after: "But we have not received the spirit of this world, but the spirit which is of God."[11] And for this cause he saith: "That eye hath not seen, nor ear heard, nor hath it ascended into the heart of man, those things which God hath prepared for them that love Him, but God hath revealed to us by His Spirit."[12]

PETER.—If then the mysteries of God were revealed to the same Apostle by the Spirit of God, why did he then, in treating of this question, set down these words beforehand, saying: "O the depth of the riches of the wisdom and knowledge of God: how incomprehensible be His judgments, and His ways investigable?"[13] And again, while I am thus speaking of this matter, another question cometh to my mind: for the prophet David said to our Lord: "With my lips have I uttered all the judgments of Thy mouth,"[14] wherefore, seeing it is less to know than to utter, what is the reason that St Paul affirmeth the judgments of God to be incomprehensible, and yet David saith that he did not only know them, but also with his lips did pronounce them?

GREGORY.—To both these questions I have already briefly answered, when I said holy men, in that they be one with our Lord, are not ignorant of the sense of our Lord. For all such as do devoutly follow our Lord be also by devotion one with our

---

[10] Ibid.

[11] Ibid.

[12] 1 Cor. ii.

[13] Rom. ix.

[14] Psalm cxviii.

Lord, and yet for all this, in that they are laden with the burden of their corruptible flesh, they be not with God: and so, in that they be joined with Him they know the secret judgments of God; and in that they be separated from God they know them not: for seeing they do not as yet perfectly penetrate His secret mysteries, they give testimony that His judgments be incomprehensible. But those that do with their soul adhere unto Him, and cleaving unto the sayings of the Holy Scripture, or to secret revelations, acknowledge what they receive; such persons both know these things and do utter them: for those judgments which God doth conceal they know not; and those which He doth utter they know: and therefore the prophet David, when he had said: "I have with my lips uttered all the judgments," he added immediately, "of Thy mouth"; as though he should plainly say: those judgments I may both know and utter which I knew Thou didst speak: for those things which Thou dost not speak without all question Thou dost conceal from our knowledge. Wherefore the sayings of David and St Paul agree together; for the judgments of God are incomprehensible; and yet those which Himself with His own mouth vouchsafed to speak are uttered with men's tongues, because men may come to the knowledge of them; and being revealed, they may be uttered, and by no means can be kept secret.

PETER.——Now I see the answer to my question. But I pray you to proceed, if anything yet remaineth to be told of his virtue and miracles.

✠

Chapter XVII

How the man of God, Benedict, did foretell the suppression of one of his own Abbeys

A certain nobleman called Theopropus, was by the good counsel of Benedict converted, who for his virtue and merit of life was very intrinsical and familiar with him. This man upon a day, coming into his cell, found him weeping very bitterly, and having expected a good while, and yet not seeing him to make an end (for the man of God used not in his prayers to weep, but rather to be sad), he demanded the cause of that his so great heaviness, to whom he answered straightway, saying: "All this Abbey which I have built, and all such things as I have made ready for my brethren, are by the judgment of Almighty God delivered to the Gentiles, to be spoiled and overthrown: and scarce could I obtain of God to have their lives spared that should then live in it." His words Theopropus then heard, but we see them to be proved most true, who know that very Abbey to be now suppressed by the Lombards. For not long since, in the night time when the monks were asleep, they entered in and spoiled all things, but yet not one man could they retain there; and so Almighty God fulfilled what He promised to His faithful servant; for though He gave them the house and all the goods, yet did He preserve their lives. In which thing I see that Benedict imitated St Paul, whose ship, though it lost[15] all the goods, yet, for his comfort, he had the lives of all that were in his company bestowed upon him, so that no one man was cast away.

---

[15] Acts xxxii.

✠

Chapter XVIII

How blessed Benedict knew the hiding away of a flagon of wine

Upon a certain time, Exhilaratus, our monk, a lay-brother, whom you know, was sent by his master to the monastery of the man of God, to carry him two wooden bottles, commonly called flagons, full of wine: who in the way, as he was going, hid one of them in a bush for himself, and presented the other to venerable Benedict, who took it very thankfully: and when the man was going away, he gave him this warning: "Take heed, my son," quoth he, "that thou drinkest not of that flagon which thou hast hidden in the bush: but first be careful to bow it down, and thou shalt find what is within it." The poor man, thus pitifully confounded by the man of God, went his way, and coming back to the place where the flagon was hidden, and desirous to try the truth of that which was told him, as he was bowing it down, a snake straightway leaped forth. Then Exhilaratus perceiving what was gotten into the wine, began to be afraid of that wickedness which he had committed.

Chapter XIX

How the man of God knew that one of his monks had received certain handkerchiefs

Not far from his Abbey there was a village, in which very many men had, by the sermons of Benedict, been converted from idolatry to the true faith of Christ. Certain nuns also there were in the same town, to whom he did often send some of his monks to preach unto them, for the good of their souls. Upon a day, one that was sent, after he had made an end of his exhortations, by the entreaty of the nuns took certain small napkins, and hid them for his own use in his bosom: whom, upon his return to the Abbey, the man of God very sharply rebuked, saying: "How cometh it to pass, brother, that sin is entered into your bosom?" At which words the monk was much amazed, for he had quite forgotten what he had put there; and therefore knew not any cause why he should deserve that reprehension: whereupon the holy man spake unto him in plain terms, and said: "Was not I present when you took the handkerchiefs of the nuns, and put them up in your bosom for your own private use?" The monk, hearing this, fell down at his feet, and was sorry that he had behaved himself so indiscreetly: forth he drew those napkins from his bosom, and threw them all away.

Chapter XX

How holy Benedict knew the proud thought of one of his monks

Upon a time, while the venerable father was at supper one of his monks, who was the son of a great man, held the candle: and as he was standing there, and the other at his meat, he began to entertain a proud cogitation in his mind, and to speak thus within himself: "Who is he that I thus wait upon at supper, and hold him the candle? And who am I that I should do him any such service?" Upon which thought straightway the holy man turned himself, and with severe reprehension spake thus unto him: "Sign your heart, brother, for what is it that you say? Sign your heart": and forthwith he called another of the monks, and bade him take the candle out of his hands, and commanded him to give over his waiting, and to repose himself: who being demanded of the monks what it was that he thought, told them how inwardly he swelled with pride, and what he spake against the man of God, secretly in his own heart. Then they all saw very well that nothing could be hidden from venerable Benedict, seeing the very sound of men's inward thoughts came unto his ears.

Chapter XXI

Of two hundred bushels of meal found before the man of God's cell

At another time there was a great dearth in the same country of Campania, so that all kind of people tasted of the misery: and all the wheat of Benedict's monastery was spent, and likewise all the bread, so that there remained no more than five loaves for dinner. The venerable man, beholding the monks sad, both rebuked them modestly for their pusillanimity, and again did comfort them with this promise: "Why," quoth he, "are you so grieved in your minds for lack of bread? Indeed, today some want there is, but tomorrow you shall have plenty": and so it fell out; for the next day two hundred bushels of meal were found in sacks before his cell door, which Almighty God sent them: but by whom, or what means, that is unknown to this very day: which miracle when the monks saw, they gave God thanks, and by this learned, in want not to make any doubt of plenty.

PETER.—Tell me, I pray you, whether this servant of God had always the spirit of prophecy, when himself pleased, or only at certain times?

GREGORY.—The spirit of prophecy doth not always illuminate the minds of the prophets; because, as it is written of the Holy Ghost that "He breatheth where He will,"[16] so we are also to know that He doth breathe likewise for what cause, and when He pleaseth. And hereof it cometh, that when King David demanded of Nathan[17] whether he might build a temple for the honour of God, the prophet Nathan gave his consent, and yet afterwards utterly forbade it. From hence likewise it proceedeth that when Eliseus saw the woman weeping, and knew not the cause, he said to his servant that did trouble her: "Let her alone, for her soul is in grief, and God hath concealed it from me and hath not told me."[18] Which thing Almighty God of great piety so disposeth: for giving at some times the spirit of prophecy, and at other times withdrawing it, He doth both lift up the prophets' minds on high, and yet doth preserve them in humility: that by the gift of the Spirit they may know what they are by God's grace, and at other times, destitute of the same Spirit may understand what they are of themselves.

PETER.—There is very great reason for that you say. But, I pray you, let me hear more of the venerable man Benedict, if there be anything else that cometh to your remembrance.

---

[16] John iii.

[17] 1 Paralip. b. xvii.

[18] 4 Kings, c. iv.

Chapter XXII

How by vision venerable Benedict disposed the building of the Abbey of Terracina

At another time he was desired by a certain virtuous man to build an abbey for his monks, upon his ground, not far from the city of Terracina. The holy man was content, and appointed an Abbot and Prior, with diverse monks under them, and when they were departing, he promised that upon such a day he would come and show them in what place the oratory should be made, and where the refectory should stand, and all the other necessary rooms: and so they, taking his blessing, went their way; and against the day appointed, which they greatly expected, they made all such things ready as were necessary to entertain him, and those that should come in his company. But the very night before, the man of God in sleep appeared to the Abbot and the Prior, and particularly described to them where each place and office was to be builded. And when they were both risen, they conferred together what either of them had seen in their sleep: but yet not giving full credit to that vision, they expected the man of God himself in person, according to his promise. But when they saw that he came not they returned back unto him very sorrowfully, saying: "We expected, father, that you should have come according to promise, and told us where each place should have been built which yet you did not." To whom he answered: "Why say you so, good brethren? Did not I come, as I promised you?" And when they asked at what time it was: "Why," quoth he, "did not I appear to either of you in your sleep, and appoint how and where every place was to be built? Go your way, and according to that platform which you then saw, build up the abbey." At which words they much marvelled, and returning back, they caused it to be built in such sort as they had been taught of him by revelation.

PETER. — Gladly would I learn by what means that could be done: to wit that he should go so far to tell them that thing in their sleep, which they should both hear and know by vision.

GREGORY. — Why do you, Peter, seek out and doubt in what manner this thing was done? For certain it is that the soul is of a more noble nature than the body. And by authority of Scripture we know that the prophet Habacuc was carried from Judaea with that dinner which he had, and was suddenly set in Chaldea[19]; by which meat the prophet Daniel was relieved: and presently afterward was brought back again to Judaea. If then, Habacuc could in a moment, with his body, go so far, and carry provision

---

[19] Dan. xiv.

How Benedict disposed the building of Terracina

for another man's dinner; what marvel is it if the holy father, Benedict, obtained grace to go in spirit, and to inform the souls of his brethren, that were asleep, concerning such things as were necessary: and that, as Habacuc about corporal meat went corporally, so Benedict should go spiritually about the despatch of spiritual business?

PETER.——I confess that your words have satisfied my doubtful mind. But I would know what manner of man he was in his ordinary talk and conversation.

Chapter XXIII

Of certain nuns absolved after their death

GREGORY.—His common talk, Peter, was usually full of virtue: for his heart conversed so above in heaven, that no words could in vain proceed from his mouth. And if at any time he spake aught, yet not as one that determined what was best to be done, but only in a threatening manner, his speech in that case was so effectual and forcible, as though he had not doubtfully or uncertainly, but assuredly pronounced and given sentence. For not far from his Abbey, there lived two nuns in a place by themselves, born of worshipful parentage, whom a religious good man did serve for the despatch of their outward business. But as nobility of family doth in some breed ignobility of mind, and maketh them in conversation to show less humility, because they remember still what superiority they had above others: even so it was with these nuns: for they had not yet learned to temper their tongues, and keep them under with the bridle of their habit; for often did they, by their indiscreet speech, provoke the aforesaid religious man to anger; who having borne with them a long time, at length he complained to the man of God, and told him with what reproachful words they entreated him: whereupon he sent them by-and-by this message, saying: "Amend your tongues, otherwise I do excommunicate you": which sentence of excommunication notwithstanding, he did not then presently pronounce against them, but only threatened if they amended not themselves. But they, for all this, changed their conditions nothing at all: both which, not long after departed this life, and were buried in the church; and when solemn Mass was celebrated in the same church, and the deacon, according to custom, said with a loud voice: "If any there be that do not communicate, let them depart," the nurse, which used to give unto our Lord an offering for them, beheld them at that time to rise out of their graves, and to depart the church.

Having oftentimes, at those words of the deacon, seen them leave the church, and that they could not tarry within, she remembered what message the man of God sent them while they were yet alive. For he told them that he did deprive them of the communion, unless they did amend their tongues and conditions. Then, with great sorrow the whole matter was signified to the man of God, who straightway with his own hands gave an oblation, saying: "Go your ways, and cause this to be offered unto our Lord for them, and they shall not remain any longer excommunicate": which oblation being offered for them, and the deacon, as he used, crying out, that such as did not communicate should depart, they were not seen any more to go out of the church: whereby

Of certain nuns absolved after their death

it was certain, that seeing they did not depart with them which did not communicate that they had received the communion of our Lord by the hands of His servant.

PETER.— It is very strange that you report: for how could he, though a venerable and most holy man, yet living in mortal body, loose those souls, which stood now before the invisible judgment of God?

GREGORY.— Was he not yet, Peter, mortal, that heard from our Saviour: "Whatsoever thou shalt bind upon earth it shall be bound also in the heavens: and whatsoever thou shalt loose in earth shall be loosed also in the heavens?"[20] Whose place of binding and loosing those have at this time, who by faith and virtuous life possess the place of holy government: and to bestow such power upon earthly men the Creator of heaven and earth descended from heaven to earth: and that flesh might judge of spiritual things, God, Who for man's sake was made flesh, vouchsafed to bestow upon him: for from thence our weakness did rise up above itself, from whence the strength of God was weakened under itself.

PETER.— For the virtue of his miracles your words do yield a very good reason.

---

[20] Matt. xvi.

Chapter XXIV

Of a boy that, after his burial, was cast out of his grave

GREGORY.—Upon a certain day, a young boy that was a monk, loving his parents more than reason would, went from the Abbey to their house, not craving the father's blessing beforehand, and the same day that he came home unto them, he departed this life: and being buried, his body, the next day after, was found cast out of the grave; which they caused again to be put in, and again the day following, they found it as before. Then in great haste they went to the man of God, fell down at his feet, and with many tears besought him that he would vouchsafe him that was dead of his favour. To whom the man of God, with his own hands delivered the holy communion of our Lord's Body, saying: "Go, and lay with great reverence this our Lord's Body upon his breast, and so bury him": which when they had done, the dead corpse after that remained quietly in the grave. By which you perceive, Peter, of what merit he was with our Lord Jesus Christ, seeing the earth would not give entertainment to his body, who departed this world out of Benedict's favour.

PETER.—I perceive it very well, and do wonderfully admire it.

Chapter XXV

How a monk, forsaking the Abbey, met with a dragon in the way

GREGORY.—A certain monk there was, so inconstant and fickle of mind, that he would needs give over the Abbey; for which fault of his the man of God did daily rebuke him, and oftentimes gave him good admonitions; but yet, for all this, by no means would he tarry amongst them, and therefore, continual suit he made that he might be discharged. The venerable man, upon a time, wearied with his importunity, in anger bade him depart; who was no sooner out of the Abbey-gate, but he found a dragon in the way, expecting him with open mouth, which being about to devour him, he began in great fear and trembling to cry out aloud, saying: "Help! help! For this dragon will eat me up." At which noise the monks running out dragon they saw none, but finding him there shaking and trembling, they brought him back again to the Abbey who forthwith promised, that he would never more forsake the monastery; and so, ever

The Little Flowers of Saint Benedict

after, he continued in his profession: for by the prayers of the holy man, he saw the dragon coming against him, whom before, when he saw not, he did willingly follow.

Chapter XXVI

How holy Benedict cured a boy of the leprosy

But I must not here pass over with silence that which I had by relation of the honourable man, Anthony, who said that his father's boy was so pitifully punished with a leprosy, that all his hair fell off, his body swelled, and filthy corruption did openly come forth. Who, being sent by his father to the man of God, he was by him quickly restored to his former health.

Chapter XXVII

How Benedict found money miraculously to relieve a poor man

Neither is that to be omitted, which one of his disciples, called Peregrinus, used to tell; for he said, that upon a certain day, an honest man, who was in debt, found no other means to help himself, but thought it his best way to acquaint the man of God with his necessity: whereupon he came to the Abbey, and finding the servant of Almighty God, gave him to understand how he was troubled by his creditor for twelve shillings which he did owe him. To whom the venerable man said that himself had not so much money; yet giving him comfortable words, he said: "Go your way, and after two days come to me again, for I can not presently help you": in which two days, after his manner, he bestowed himself in prayer, and when upon the third day the poor man came back, there were found suddenly upon the chest of the Abbey, which was full of corn, thirteen shillings, which the man of God caused to be given to him that required but twelve, both to discharge his debt, and also to defray his own charges.

But now will I return to speak of such things as I had from the mouth of his own scholars mentioned before in the beginning of this book. A certain man there was, who had an enemy that did notably spite and malign him, whose damnable hatred proceeded so far that he poisoned his drink: which, although it killed him not, yet did it change his skin in such sort that it was of many colours, as though he had been infected with a leprosy: but the man of God restored him to his former health: for so soon as he touched him, forthwith all that variety of colours departed from his body.

Chapter XXVIII

How a cruet of glass was thrown upon the stones, and not broken

At such time as there was a great dearth in Campania, the man of God had given away all the wealth of the Abbey to poor people; so that in the cellar there was nothing left but a little oil in a glass. A certain sub-deacon, called Agapitus, came unto him, instantly craving that he would bestow a little oil upon him. Our Lord's servant, that was resolved to give away all upon earth, that he might find all in heaven, commanded that oil to be given him: but the monk that kept the cellar heard what the father commanded yet did he not perform it: who, inquiring, not long after, whether he had given that which he willed, the monk told him that he had not, adding that if he had given it away, that there was not any left for the Convent. Then in an anger he commanded others to take that glass with the oil, and to throw it out at the window, to the end that nothing might remain in the Abbey contrary to obedience. The monks did so, and threw it out at a window under which there was a huge downfall, full of rough and craggy stones, upon which the glass did light, but yet continued for all that so sound as though it had never been thrown out at all; for neither the glass was broken, nor any of the oil shed. Then the man of God did command it to be taken up again, and whole as it was, to be given unto him that desired it, and in the presence of the other brethren he reprehended the disobedient monk, both for his infidelity, and also for his proud mind.

Chapter XXIX

How an empty barrel was filled with oil

After which reprehension, with the rest of his brethren, he fell to praying; and in the place where they were, there stood an empty barrel with a cover upon it: and as the holy man continued in his prayers, the oil within did so increase that the cover began to be lifted up, and at length fell down; and the oil, that was now higher than the mouth of the barrel, began to run over the pavement, which so soon as the servant of God, Benedict, beheld, forthwith he gave over his prayer, and the oil likewise ceased to overflow the barrel. Then did he more at large admonish that mistrusting and disobedient monk, that he would learn to have faith and humility; who, upon so wholesome an admonition, was ashamed; because the venerable father had by miracle shown the power of Almighty God, as before he told him when he did first rebuke him: and so no cause there was why any should afterward doubt of His promise; seeing at one and the same time for a small glass almost empty which he gave away, He bestowed upon them a whole barrel full of oil.

Chapter XXX

How Benedict delivered a monk from a devil

Upon a certain time, as he was going to the Oratory of St John, which is in the top of the mountain, the old enemy of mankind, upon a mule, like a physician, met him, carrying in his hand a horn and a mortar. And when he demanded whither he was going: "To your monks," quoth he, "to give them a drench." The venerable father went forward to his prayers, and when he had done, he returned in all haste: but the wicked spirit found an old monk drawing of water, into whom he entered, and straightway cast him upon the ground, and grievously tormented him. The man of God, coming from his prayers, and seeing him in such pitiful case, gave him only a little blow with his hand, and at the same instant he cast out that cruel devil, so that he durst not any more presume to enter in.

The Little Flowers of Saint Benedict

PETER.—I would gladly know whether he obtained always by prayer to work such notable miracles; or else sometimes did them only at his will and pleasure.

GREGORY.—Such as be the devout servants of God, when necessity requireth, use to work miracles both manner of ways: so that sometimes they effect wonderful things by their prayers, and sometimes only by their power and authority: for St John saith: "So many as received Him He gave them power to be made the sons of God."[21] They, then, that by power be the sons of God, what marvel is it, if by power they be able to do wonderful things. And that both ways they work miracles, we learn of St Peter,[22] who by his prayers did raise up Tabitha, and by his sharp reprehension did sentence Ananias and Saphira to death for their lying. For we read not that in the death of them he prayed at all, but only rebuked them for that sin which they had committed. Certain therefore it is, that sometimes they do these things by power, and sometimes by prayer, for Ananias and Saphira by a severe rebuke St Peter deprived of life, and by prayer restored Tabitha to life. And for proof of this, I will now tell you of two miracles which the faithful servant of God, Benedict, did, in which it shall appear most plainly that he wrought the one by that power which God gave him, and obtained the other by virtue of his prayers.

---

[21] 1 John i.
[22] Acts ix. 5.

How the devil disguised as a physician met St Benedict

✠

Chapter XXXI

Of a country fellow, that, with the only sight of the man of God, was loosed from his bonds

A certain Goth there was, called Zalla, an Arian heretic, who, in the time of King Totila, did with such monstrous cruelty persecute religious men of the Catholic Church, that what priest or monk soever came in his presence, he never departed alive. This man, on a certain day, set upon rapine and pillage, pitifully tormented a poor countryman, to make him confess where his money and wealth was: who, overcome with extremity of pain, said that he had committed all his substance to the custody of Benedict, the servant of God: and this he did to the end that his tormentor, giving credit to his words, might, at least for a while, surcease from his horrible cruelty. Zalla, hearing this, tormented him no longer: but binding his arms fast with strong cords, drave him before his horse, to bring him unto this Benedict, who, as he said, had his wealth in keeping. The country fellow, thus pinioned, and running before him, carried him to the holy man's abbey, where he found him sitting before the gate, reading upon a book. Then turning back to Zalla, that came raging after, he said: "This is Father Benedict, of whom I told you": who looking upon him, in a great fury, thinking to deal as terribly with him as he had with others, cried out aloud to him, saying: "Rise up, sirrah, rise up, and deliver me quickly such wealth as thou hast of this man's in keeping." The man of God, hearing such a noise, straightway lifted up his eyes from reading, and beheld both him and the country fellow; and turning his eyes to his bands, very strangely they fell from his arms, and that so quickly as no man with any haste could have undone them. Zalla, seeing him so wonderfully and quickly loosed, fell straight a-trembling, and prostrating himself upon the earth, bowed down his cruel and stiff neck to the holy man's feet, and with humility did commend himself to his prayers. But the venerable man, for all this, rose not up from his reading, but calling for some of his monks, commanded them to have him in, and to give him some meat. And when he was brought back again he gave him a good lesson, admonishing him not to use any more such rigour and cruel dealing. His proud mind thus taken down, away he went, but durst not demand after that anything of the country fellow, whom the man of God, not with hands, but only with his eyes, had loosed from his bands. And this is that, Peter, which I told you, that those which in a more familiar sort serve God, do sometimes, by a certain power and authority bestowed upon them, work miracles. For he that, sitting still, did appease

Of a country fellow that was loosed from his bonds

the fury of that cruel Goth and unloose with his eyes those knots and cords which did pinion the innocent man's arms, did plainly show by the quickness of the miracle that he had received power to work all that which he did. And now will I likewise tell you of another miracle, which by prayer he obtained at God's hands.

✠

Chapter XXXII

How by prayer venerable Benedict raised up a dead child

B eing upon a day gone out with his monks to work in the field, a countryman carrying the corpse of his dead son came to the gate of the Abbey, lamenting the loss of his child; and inquiring for holy Benedict, they told him that he was abroad with his monks in the field. Down at the gate he laid the dead body, and with great sorrow of soul ran in haste to seek out the venerable father. At the same time, the man of God was returning homeward from work with his monks, whom so soon as he saw, he began to cry out: "Give me my son—give me my son!" The man of God, amazed at these words, stood still and said: "What! have I taken away your son?" "No, no," quoth the sorrowful father, "but he is dead: come for Christ Jesus' sake and restore him to life." The servant of God, hearing him speak in that manner, and seeing his monks upon compassion to solicit the poor man's suit, with great sorrow of mind he said: "Away, my good brethren, away: such miracles are not for us to work, but for the blessed Apostles: why will you lay such a burden upon me as my weakness cannot bear?" But the poor man, whom excessive grief enforced, would not give over his petition, but swore that he would never depart except he did raise up his son. "Where is he, then?" quoth God's servant: he answered that his body lay at the gate of the Abbey: to which place when the man of God came with his monks, he knelt down and lay upon the body of the little child, and rising, he held up his hands towards heaven, and said: "Behold not, O Lord, my sins, but the faith of this man, that desireth to have his son raised to life: and restored that soul to the body which Thou hast taken away." He had scarce spoken these words, and behold the soul returned back again, and therewith the child's body began to tremble in such sort that all which were present did behold it in strange manner to pant and shake. Then he took it by the hand, and gave it to his father, but alive and in health. Certain it is, Peter, that this miracle was not in his own power, for which prostrate upon the ground he prayed so earnestly.

PETER.—All is most true that before you said, for what you affirmed in words you have now verified by examples and works. But tell me, I beseech you, whether holy men can do all such things as they please, and obtain at God's hands whatsoever they desire.

Chapter XXXIII

Of a miracle wrought by his sister, Scholastica

GREGORY.—What man is there, Peter, in this world, that is in greater favour with God than St Paul was? who yet three times desired our Lord to be delivered from the pricks of the flesh, and obtained not his petition.[23] Concerning which point also, I must needs tell you, how there was one thing which the venerable father Benedict would have done, and yet he could not. For his sister, called Scholastica, dedicated from her infancy to our Lord, used once a year to come and visit her brother. To whom the man of God went not far from the gate, to a place that did belong to the Abbey, there to give her entertainment. And she, coming thither on a time, according to her custom, her venerable brother with his monks went to meet her, where they spent the whole day in the praises of God and spiritual

---

[23] 2 Cor. xii.

talk, and when it was almost night they supped together, and as they were yet sitting at the table, talking of devout matters, and darkness came on, the holy nun, his sister, entreated him to stay there all night, that they might spend it in discoursing of the joys of heaven. But by no persuasion would he agree unto that, saying that he might not by any means tarry all night out of his Abbey. At that time the sky was so clear that no cloud was to be seen. The nun, receiving this denial of her brother, joining her hands together, laid them upon the table; and so, bowing down her head upon them, she made her prayers to Almighty God, and lifting her head from the table, there fell suddenly such a tempest of lightning and thundering, and such abundance of rain, that neither venerable Benedict nor his monks that were with him, could put their head out of doors: for the holy nun resting her head upon her hands, poured forth such a flood of tears upon the table that she drew the clear air to a watery sky, so that after the end of her devotions, that storm of rain followed; and her prayer and the rain did so meet together, that as she lifted up her head from the table, the thunder began, so that in one and the very same instant she lifted up her head and brought down the rain. The man of God, seeing that he could not by reason of such thunder and lightning, and great abundance of rain, return back to his Abbey, began to be heavy, and to complain of his sister, saying: "God forgive you, what have you done?" to whom she answered: "I desired you to stay, and you would not hear me; I have desired our good Lord, and He hath vouchsafed to grant my petition: wherefore if you can now depart, in God's name return to your monastery, and leave me here alone." But the good father, not being able to go

Of a miracle wrought by his sister, Scholastica

forth, tarried there against his will, where willingly before he would not stay. And so by that means they watched all night, and with spiritual and heavenly talk did mutually comfort one another: and therefore, by this we see, as I said before, that he would have that thing which yet he could not: for if we respect the venerable man's mind, no question but he would have had the same fair weather to have continued as it was when he set forth, but he found that a miracle did prevent his desire, which by the power of Almighty God a woman's prayers had wrought. And it is not a thing to be marvelled at that a woman which of long time had not seen her brother, might do more at that time than he could, seeing according to the saying of St John,[24] "God is charity": and therefore of right she did more which loved more.

PETER. — I confess that I am wonderfully pleased with that which you tell me.

---

[24] 1 John iv.

How St Benedict discoursed for the last time with St Scholastica

Chapter XXXIV

How Benedict saw the soul of his sister ascend into heaven

GREGORY.—The next day the venerable woman returned to her nunnery, and the man of God to his Abbey: who three days after, standing in his cell, and lifting up his eyes to heaven, beheld the soul of his sister, which was departed from her body, in the likeness of a dove to ascend into heaven: who rejoicing much to see her great glory, with hymns and lauds gave thanks to Almighty God, and did impart the news of this her death to his monks, whom also he sent presently to bring her corpse to his Abbey, to have it buried in that grave which he provided for himself. By means whereof it fell out that as their souls were always one in God whilst they lived, so their bodies continued together after their death.

Chapter XXXV

How he saw the whole world represented before his eyes, and also the soul of Germanus, Bishop of Capua, ascending to heaven

At another time, Servandus, the deacon, and Abbot of that monastery, which in times past was founded by the noble man Liberius, in the country of Campania, used ordinarily to come and visit the man of God: and the reason why he came so often was because himself also was a man full of heavenly doctrine; and so they two had often together spiritual conference, to the end that albeit they could not perfectly feed upon the celestial food of heaven, yet, by means of such sweet discourses, they might at least, with longing and fervent desire, taste of those joys and divine delights. When it was time to go to rest, the venerable father Benedict reposed himself in the top of a tower, at the foot whereof Servandus the deacon was lodged, so that one pair of stairs went to them both: before the tower there was a certain large room in which both their disciples did lie. The man of God, Benedict, being diligent in watching, rose up early, before the time of matins (his monks being yet at rest), and came to the window of his chamber, where he offered up his prayers to Almighty God. Standing there, all on a sudden, in the dead of the night, as he looked forth, he saw a light which banished away the darkness of the night, and glittered with such brightness, that the light which did shine in the midst of the darkness was far more clear than the light of the day. Upon this sight a marvellous strange thing followed, for as himself did afterward report, the whole world, gathered as it were together under one beam of the sun, was presented before his eyes, and whilst the venerable father stood attentively beholding the brightness of that glittering light, he saw the soul of Germanus, Bishop of Capua, in a fiery globe to be carried up by Angels into heaven. Then, desirous to have some witness of this so notable a miracle, he called with a very loud voice Servandus the Deacon, twice or thrice by his name, who, troubled at such an unusual crying out of the man of God, went up in all haste, and looking forth, saw not anything else but a little remnant of the light, but wondering at so great a miracle, the man of God told him all in order what he had seen, and sending by-and-by to the town of Cassino, he commanded the religious man, Theopropus, to despatch one that night to the city of Capua, to learn what was become of Germanus their Bishop; which being done, the messenger found that reverend Prelate departed this life; and inquiring curiously the time, he

How he saw the whole world represented before his eyes

understood that he died at that very instant in which the man of God beheld him ascending up to heaven.

PETER.—A strange thing, and very much to be admired. But whereas you say that the whole world, as it were under one sunbeam, was presented before his eyes, as I must needs confess that in myself I never had experience of any such thing, so neither can I conceive by what means the whole world can be seen of any one man.

GREGORY.—Assure yourself, Peter, of that which I speak, to wit, that all creatures be, as it were, nothing, to that soul which beholdeth the Creator: for though it see but a glimpse of that light which is in the Creator, yet very small do all things seem that be created: for by means of that supernatural light the capacity of the inward soul is enlarged, and is in God so extended that it is far above the world: yea, and the soul of him that seeth in this manner is also above itself; for being rapt up in the light of God, it is inwardly in itself enlarged above itself; and when it is so exalted, and looketh downward, then doth it comprehend how little all that is which before in former baseness it could not comprehend.

The man of God, therefore, who saw the fiery globe, and the Angels returning to heaven, out of all doubt could not see those things but in the light of God: what marvel, then, is it, if he saw the world gathered together before him, who, rapt up in the light of his soul, was at that time out of the world. But albeit we say that the world was gathered together before his eyes, yet heaven and earth were not drawn into any lesser room than they be of themselves, but the soul of the beholder was more enlarged, which, rapt in God, might without difficulty see that which is under God, and therefore in that light which appeared to his outward eyes, the inward light which was in his soul ravished the mind of the beholder to supernal things, and showed him how small all earthly things were.

PETER. — I perceive now that it was more to my profit that I understood you not before: seeing, by reason of my slow capacity, you have delivered so notable an exposition. But now, because you have made me thoroughly to understand these things, I beseech you to continue on your former narration.

Chapter XXXVI

How holy Benedict wrote a rule for his monks

Desirous I am, Peter, to tell you many things of this venerable father, but some of purpose I let pass, because I make haste to treat also of the acts of other holy men: yet I would not have you to be ignorant, but that the man of God amongst so many miracles for which he was so famous in the world, was also sufficiently learned in divinity, for he wrote a rule for his monks, both excellent for discretion, and also eloquent for the style. Of whose life and conversation, if any be curious to know further, he may in the institution of that rule understand all his manner of life and discipline: for the holy man could not otherwise teach than himself lived.

Chapter XXXVII

How venerable Benedict did prophesy to his monks the time of his own death

The same year in which he departed this life he told the day of his holy death to his monks, some of which did live daily with him, and some dwelt far off, willing those that were present to keep it secret, and telling those that were absent by what token they should know that he was dead. Six days before he left this world he gave orders to have his sepulchre opened, and forthwith falling into an ague, he began with burning heat to wax faint; and whenas the sickness daily increased, upon the sixth day he commanded his monks to carry him into the oratory, where he did arm himself with receiving the Body and Blood of our Saviour, Christ; and having his weak body holden up betwixt the hands of his disciples, he stood with his own lifted up to heaven; and as he was in that manner praying, he gave up the ghost. Upon which day, two monks, one being in his cell, and the other far distant, had concerning him, one and the self-same vision: for they saw all the way from the holy man's cell, towards the east even up to heaven, hung and adorned with tapestry, and shining with an infinite number of lamps; at the top whereof a man reverently attired stood, and demanded if they knew who passed that way; to whom they answered, saying that they knew not. Then he spake unto them, "This is the way," quoth he, "by which the beloved servant of God, Benedict, is ascended up to heaven." And by this means, as his monks that were present knew of the death of the holy man, so likewise they which were absent by the token which he foretold them, had intelligence of the same thing. Buried he was in the oratory of St John the Baptist, which himself built when he overthrew the altar of Apollo; who also in that cave in which he first dwelt, even to this very time, worketh miracles, if the faith of them that pray requireth the same.

Chapter XXXVIII

How a mad woman was cured in his cave

For the thing which I mean now to rehearse, fell out lately. A certain woman falling mad, lost the use of reason so far, that she walked up and down, day and night, in the mountains and valleys, in woods and fields, and rested only in that place where extreme weariness enforced her to stay. Upon a day, it so fell out, that albeit she wandered at random, yet she missed not the right way, for she came to the cave of the blessed man Benedict: and not knowing anything, in she went, and reposed herself there that night; and rising up in the morning she departed as sound in sense and well in her wits, as though she had never been distracted in her whole life, and so continued always after, even to her dying day.

PETER.—What is the reason that in the patronage of martyrs we oftentimes find that they do not afford so great benefits by their bodies as they do by other of their relics, and do there work greater miracles where themselves be not present?

The Little Flowers of Saint Benedict

GREGORY.—Where the holy martyrs lie in their bodies, there is no doubt, Peter, but that they are able to work many miracles, yea, and also do work infinite, to such as seek them with a pure mind. But forasmuch as simple people might have some doubt whether they be present, and do in those places hear their prayers where their bodies be not, necessary it is that they should in those places show greater miracles where weak souls may most doubt of their presence. But he whose mind is fixed in God hath so much the greater merit of his faith, in that he both knoweth that they rest not there in body, and yet be there present to hear our prayers. And therefore our Saviour Himself, to increase the faith of His disciples, said: "If I do not depart, the Comforter will not come unto you":[25] for, seeing that it is certain that the comforting Spirit doth always proceed from the Father and the Son, why doth the Son say that He will depart, that the Comforter may come, Who never is absent from the Son? But because the disciples, beholding our Lord in the flesh, did always desire to see Him with their corporal eyes, very well did He say unto them: "Unless I do go away the Comforter will not come": as though He had plainly told them: If I do not withdraw My Body, I cannot let you understand what the love of the Spirit is: and except you give over to love My carnal Presence, never will you learn to affect Me with true spiritual love.

PETER.—What you say pleaseth me very well.

---

[25] John xvi.

How a mad woman was cured in his cave

GREGORY. — Let us now for a while give over our discourse, to the end that if we mean to prosecute the miracles of other saints, we may through silence be the more able to perform it.

About The Cenacle Press at Silverstream Priory

An apostolate of the Benedictine monastery of Silverstream Priory in Ireland, the mission of The Cenacle Press can be summed up in four words: *Quis ostendit nobis bona*—who will show us good things (Psalm 4:6)? In an age of confusion, ugliness, and sin, our aim is to show something of the Highest Good to every reader who picks up our books. More specifically, we believe that the treasury of the centuries-old Benedictine tradition and the beauty of holiness which has characterized so many of its followers through the ages has something beneficial, worthwhile, and encouraging in it for every believer.

cenaclepress.com

Also available from The Cenacle Press at Silverstream Priory

Robert Hugh Benson
The King's Achievement
By What Authority
The Friendship of Christ
Papers of a Pariah
Christ in the Church

Blessed Columba Marmion OSB
Christ the Ideal of the Monk
Christ in His Mysteries
Words of Life On the Margin of the Missal

Dom Pius De Hemptinne OSB
A Benedictine Soul: Biography, Letters, and Spiritual Writings of Dom Pius De Hemptinne

Dom Hubert Van Zeller OSB
Letters to A Soul
We Work While the Light Lasts
Approach to Penance
Sanctity in Other Words

Dom Eugene Vandeur OSB
Hail Mary

Father Ryan T Sliwa
New Nazareth's In Us

Monks of Silverstream Priory
Dawn Tears, Spring Light, Rood Peace: Poems

cenaclepress.com

www.ingramcontent.com/pod-product-compliance
Lightning Source LLC
Chambersburg PA
CBHW030305100526
44590CB00012B/522